ON A BLUE STAR

REMEMBER WHO YOU ARE

RAIN RIVER AND OCEAN HEART

WIND, AND FREE AIR

STONE, BURNING ITS SOUL

OLD FIRE OF STARS

Arthur Woodlands

On A Blue Star

LYRICS

Kind Letters of the House

The book *'On a Blue Star'* is a collection of lyrical poetry. It is written on a style that mimics painters and short-moviemakers, creating a view in mind by a rhyme, connecting and bending it to a natural event or human feeling. Feeling can be – with right music and scene – breathtaking, mind bending and soul carving.

'On a Blue Star' consists of Six Sections, well maybe seven, but the last is just 'great cigarettes after sex'. Name embraces our planet and human survival on it. Themes and titles of the sections eventually provided enough gravity to hold this noble name on its orbit. And it's a good dual-logy continuation for my last book of poetry, Heart of Earth.

Trip to lyrical poetry starts humbly from moon with a lovely chapter *Moon Maidens*, and continues by mind-bending philosophy of *Rome Falls, Atlantis Soul* and *Lady EA*. Then, we come closer to everyday life by summer songs of *Summer City Sun* and strangely complicated mood songs of *Ghost Stories*. Last chapter *Little Moodies* is a collection of short cigarette or coffee moment feeling risers.

The lyrics are written between 2017 and 2022. Somewhat interestingly, the chapter *Rome Falls* and most of its lyrics were written before pandemic closed the doors of world, so to say, before 'Rome fell'.

'Soul Moon Tides' is a mood-einstein starter of the chapter *Moon Maidens*. It describes perhaps the best the theme: *mood-makers, love songs, over-natural forces, soul seeking, ladies with magical spells*; where the storytelling is aided by eyes-and-thoughts of some of the nicest gods of the great Creek mythology.

Rome Falls brings down not the lightest moods, even the lyric '*Rome Falls*' has a rhyme: '*Babe, I had a dream / Rome falling tonight*' – This is the time and place when Venus and Mars date? Except the historical sequence of events, concept has of course a philosophical aspect. Word 'Rome' is also a close relative of 'home'. And maybe, '*Rome Falls*', is a great waterfall either on your life or in the history of human civilization. Even mainly written before, the message certainly catches something essential from the strange years 2020-22. Perhaps it, the chapter, tries to reset you on the primary basic values. So, the themes are as soft as: *personal conflicts, war, extreme adventure, risk taking, leaving something valuable behind, survival, and well, there was also some serious love involved.*

Atlantis Soul – please, don't speak for thousand years! Some people claim that human being has a precious thing called soul, and famous myth tells about the lost gorgeous paradise on shores, or bottom, of the Atlantic Ocean called Atlantis. Theme has a scent of survival since it follows the fall of Rome. Additionally, it also grows, and tides, with the moon maidens already introduced. It is also elemental, the water and ocean of the four elements. Anyone sailed, dived, felt sea swells, or stared the eye of ocean horizon long enough, will understand. Over 70% of our blue star is covered by the great blue ... 'blaa blaa blue', for 24 hours. And yes, it smoothly blue-suits to Heart-of-Earth philosophy. So, the theme is something like *finding a lost soul, awakening it, natural powers, primary feelings and emotions walking on earth as mythical gods of moods.*

Lady Ea may be your lover. In this book, mother earth is still pretty young woman, a lady mistress earth. She can be referred to everything from Eve on paradise to awesome lady you know, with some superpowers of course, such as: *renaissance of heart, star gazing eyes, ocean soul, mountain cool.* Who wouldn't fall in love with this lady, even the Rome fell, moon and Adam. No need to be a monk on the Everest to get the idea, earth – human connection, everything on our evolution as a species, even from late development of African ape, has been affected by the surrounding environment. My poet likes an Indian kind of philosophy that smokes-clouds-on-sky just to confirm that all the feelings and moods are present in the natural phenomenona on our little blue star – just open your eyes, ears, what-ever-you-have and soul. Back to the theme, *Lady EA*, well you're born on it, you live on it – and you are forced to love and desire her, it is well written in your homosapien codex. She's a goddess, of hearts on earth.

Summer City Sun is a set of light and marvel summer feelings. Please, don't underestimate summer, closer to polar circles one clearly understands what it means to all life and to various hormonal activities connected to human moods, and thus also to soul. Themes go with *summer feelings, no cloths, light soundings, urban survival, heart-rising feelings and moods of summer love.* The starter, wide *'Indian summer sky' is* a brilliant summer moodie.

Ghost Stories are either focus-grouped mood-makers, or strange puzzles and riddles of heart, body, mind and soul. Maybe ghost here is a shadow of soul, left on a place of a strong feeling doomed to carry that character for the rest of life. Who knows, these are little-big tales scattered around the world.

Little Moodies are mood enhancers; suitable for a t-shirt or coffee cup print. Set of few rhymes aimed for finding some quality soul time. Check them through, not most ordinary ones, and they hold some soul strength.

A recommendation by the author

 All the lyrics were written while listening music, most while enjoying a breathtaking scene. So, choose music of your favorite with a suitable rhythm, and try to catch the soul of the artwork, mood and something mysterious inside you. Really hope that you find your favorite(s) on a specific mood or occasion. May the old Creek Gods help you!

Then, pour a wine glass through your big heart – through your
soul's desire, and hold your favorite philosopher's head,
scientist's hand, mistress' knee or grand-pa's bible tight.
Houston and Rome, here we go ... Romeo, seeking her Juliet
from the moon first.

Before you go on, there's one man you should be aware ...

> *From the Shadows of the World*
> *Man Appeared*
> *For the Humble, He Declared*
>
> *I am the Music*
> *Dance and Poetry*
> *Paintings You Live In ...*
>
> *And He Drew Off Curtains of Secret Garden*
> *Calling the Show*
> *By Swing of His Hand*
> *Now Pointing to a Faint Smile*
> *On a just Revealed Face of Moon*
>
> *And All the Nine Came*
> *Beautiful Dancers, Down from Heavens*
> *Dressed only on Shadows and Smiles*
>
> *Pour Some Wine*
> *For The Poor Souls ...*
>
> *With the Sudden Tide of the Moon*
> *Lady Wind Blew Thousand Leaves*
> *Hailing on Air*
>
> *And the Man Was Vanished*
> *Into the just Deepened Shadows of Audience*
>
> *– Among Gods –*

MOON MAIDENS

Moon ... twin, sister and brother of earth! Tides, ocean currents, survival light for the dark nights, mythical pale of the silver, shaded mirror of sun with all its lunar phases. All it's magical powers and goddess myth philosophies are hard to be explained shortly. Maybe it's better to approach the dualities dilemma by a poem

> *Houston! I think I see a Moon*
> *It draws an Ocean ... of Moods*

Actually, my personal experience that I cannot explain reasonably, whenever I start to feel emotional in any reason, I seem to take a look up the sky. And guess who's there, my wise and humble goddess moon ... an young crescent on light blue of middle day, or waning gibbon raising a silver bridge over serene waters, or best, a full goddess-eye leaned closer with intensive exotic mood that makes anything else smaller and meaningless ... emotional gravity. At this phase of the story, I would like to call to a one man called Newton, sitting under a paradise apple tree during a blue moment with a full moonlight. Most likely, the apple does not hit the Newton's head, but more likely a snake in a tree. This is maybe, because of the presence of *gravital effects of the moon.* I've even heard a theory that this 'emotional gravity' could be better described by other fruit than bible-apple. So, think two romantic scientists, lovers, sitting below, for example, a banana tree on eve's delight and full moonlight. Even in perspective of evolution, the relativity of two-body motions might have had great impact on the design of banana. Maybe bananas have curved, while trying to follow its color-twins star-shine during sun's ride across the sky. Anyway, the Banana-Newtonian experiments are of course a lullaby fairy tales, but what is worth to moon-highlight is that the goddess moon might tide our emotions, and thus also bend the feeling of

time passing by. And on these situations you may *feel your soul
– a magical experience!* Now, it is really better to move on with
the maidens.

To get you on the mood, I call upon Moon Maidens, to tide
your heart. These ladies can set your perspectives and values in
a new order. *Who are these fair ladies? Maybe you know one?*
Maybe, it's more about the spirit, way of living and seeing things.
Think of these high-spirit ladies going naked and stepping into a
pond or pool for a swim, lighted only by a full moon and stars.
'*Swimming with moon and stars*', some people carry the spirit
on everyday life.

I have met and discussed with my *Moon Maiden* before writing
the first lyric, which has the most impressive title I can feel. So,
for delight and happiness of your soul ...

Soul Moon Tides

An Ocean
Ocean of Blood
And a River, of Clouds
That Floods
Time Tides, on Hour Moon
Time Tides, on Hour Moon

Selene, Slow-Walking her Favorite Park
Colours, Gravity of Shadows
High Tide of Emotions
High Tide of Emotions

Diving, Soul Moon Diving
It's an Ocean, Ocean Red
Spilling, Spilling Dead Man's Chest

Bird Eye Circling
Pieces, of God's Dreams
And You Know It's You, Mister Moods
Looking for a Lady
Lingering in the Woods

It's an Ocean, Ocean of Blood
And a River of Clouds, Raining Down

Time Tides, as Hour Moon Stops By
Selene Slow-Mo Sails her Ark
Scent of Colours
Growing Gravity of Shadows
High Tide, Miss Moon Soul

Slow Down, Jackson
Ghost Steps, Please
Statue Dancing Moonstones

It's an Ocean, Ocean of Blood
    Swelling Sea
        Selene Slow-Surfing, on Soul Chest
And a River of Clouds, Raining Time Down

Muses of Moon

And I Heard a Call
It was Little Apollo
Handsome and Tall
"Where's Dionysus?
Tell, Takes his Violin
And there's no Dress Code
No Dress Code

It was a Female Voice
"I Know a Place
With a Dancing Floor
Where Ladies moving
Like Cats on Jungle War"

And I Had my CrossBow
But Dionysus Playing It with Silent Chords

It was a Female Voice
Dionysus, Show me Teeth and Claws
Blood's Red, Six-Teen Cents from War
Diana says She wants to Dance
And Moon Veils
Everything but its Maids
On a Tiding Floor, On a Tiding Floor

'Muses of Moon ... Muses of Moon'

They make me Crazy
They make me Fool
Dionysus, Playing Apollo's Bow
Diana wants to Dance
'Muses of a Moon'

It was a Female Voice

Honey on Butterfly
I Know a Place, with a Dancing Choice
And There's no Dress Code

And Ladies, Wearing Jungle Cat Moves
Teeth & Claws, Dionysus
Blood's Red, Six-teen Cents from War

And Moon Veils
Everything but its Maids
On a Tiding Floor, On a Tiding Floor

'Muses of Moon, Muses of Moon'

Easy Light Morning

Easy Light Morning
Hiding Under Caffeine
Let View, Fall over Me
And There's a Stranger in You
Faint Buddha Smile
Landing on Lotus Pose
Can You Feel, Edge of the World

It's an Easy Light Morning
Someone Smoking Strange Thoughts
Purpose of Life
Take a Pose, on Foundation of Philosophy

O' Holy Smoke
Long Peace before War
Breathing In, Lost Dreams
Say Hi, to Saint Shy
Riding on Dinosaur Thoughts

It's an Easy Light Morning
Hiding under Caffeine
Someone Smoking Mental Cigarette
And There's a Stranger in Your Thoughts

O' Buddha Please, Hide that Smile
Dinosaur Musing, on Lost World

It's an Easy Light Morning
Breathing in, Strange Slow Thoughts
Easy Light Morning
Laying on Surface, of Swelling Soul
Can You Feel, Edge of the World
O' Buddha Please, Hide that Smile

Easy Light Morning
Feel that Cigarette Squeeze
Mental Breeze
Someone Calls, by your Old Name
And there's a Stranger Disguised
In your Lazy Devil-Eyes

It's an Easy Light Morning
Hiding under Caffeine
Let the View, Fall Over Me

Apollo's Blind

And I Call to my Friend Blind

O' My Little Apollo
O' My Little Apollo
Have your Drink
Have your Wine
Have your F. Fine Dine

Lost my Soul ... on Day's Fight
Call my Friend, Who's Blind
O' My Little Apollo
O' My ... Apollo
Have your Drink
Have your little Dance
Have your Music
Have your Grazy Little Thoughts

Lost my Soul ... on Day's Fight
Call my Friend's Blind
O' That Apollo's ... Closed Smile

Have your Drink
Have your Dream
Have your Fallen Sky

Lost my Soul ... on Day's Night
O' my Friend Blind
Pour me some Wine
Have your Music
Have your Dance
Wear your Timeless God Mask
O' my Friend, who's Blind
Have your Drink
Have your Fun, Have your little Sun

O' my Friend who's Blind
Wearing Young Moon Smile
Lady Summer Night, Asking You for a Dance

O' my Little Apollo
Have your Music, Have your Drink
Have Your Sun Dance

She's a Boomerang Smile

I Bet ... There's a Stranger
You're Hiding Somewhere
I Bet, There's a Secret
A Bag ... Full of 'Em

I Bet ... There's a Stranger in You
Someone, You Never Met
O' I Need to Meet Her

I Bet ... She's a Secret
Dreams Hiding Her

O' Lady Little Finger
She's Miss Mystique
She's a Moon Maid
Stranger, Someone you Never Met Before
Hides a Secret
Blood Diamond, Out of Tibetan Moon

She's a Mystery, I Know
Secret Sis-Twin, Hiding under Skin
On a Distant World
Someone Dials my Name
And She Throws Boomerang Smile
Run Ostrich, Run
Run while You Can

And She Plays her Violin Walk
Music Young Aphrodite-Queen
Bohemian Jaguar
Stretching her Spinal AI

O' Lady Little Finger
She's a Secret, Muse and Mistress of Moon

And I Drink Potion of Love, Drug She Fools
It's Raining Serotonin, under Parisian Skies

I Bet, It's her Favorite Game
Need to Do Her the Same
But She Throws Her Boomerang Smile
Hey Miss Moon Maid
It's Raining Red and White
Under Parisian Sky

Philosopher Romeo

O' I'm Aching, Elbow Swollen
    It's my Philosopher
        He's Done, Thought Broken

He's Lying on Sun
O' Juliette, Divine Love
    Philosopher Romeo
        Loosing his Mind

O' He Got a Sun
    Something to Rely on

Lying on Sun
    Got Poison Called Love
        Overdose of Divine God
  He's Lying on Sun

Romeo Moonwalking, Shadows on Graveyard

He's Lying on Sun
    Got Overdose, Cupido's Shot on Heart
        Poison Called Love
   Romeo, Screaming Juliette
     She's Mistress, Moon Princess Imprisoned

Just Before Dark
    All the Eve's Apples, have an Hour Smile

O' Juliette, It's Philosopher Romeo
    Looking for Divine Love

Romeo Stumbles, on Moon-Shadows of Graveyard
    And Juliette Calls
        All her Moon Maidens for a Slow Waltz

Morning On Moon

It's Morning, on Moon
Morning on Moon
Walking on Star Avenue
On Star Avenue

It's Morning on Moon
Waving for my Blue Mood
Trees Grow over Green
Shadows Deeper, Seem to Speak Slow
Speak to my Soul

'It's Morning on Moon'

Vanity, Walks Close By
Throws Two Stones
Through your Naked Ghost
Seat for a King
Seat, for a Queen

O' It's Morning on Moon
Morning on Moon

Colours Grow Deeper
Shadows Steeper, and Seem to Speak
Dreams Flying By
Soul Stretching after Long Sleep

And Vanity Walks By
Looks You Small Far Down
Throws Two Stones
Seat for a King – Seat, for a Queen

O' Lady, Cousins with Love
She's Small, for a God
Throws a Smile

Proposes a Meeting, with Immortal

'It's Morning on Moon'

Colours Grow Deeper
Shadows, Seem to Speak Language Soul
And I Hail my Moon Stones
All my Dreams, Seem to Fly-by

'It's Morning on Moon'

Stone River

Hey, Darling Faraway
Send me a Thought
Blow it, into the Eve Breeze

And She Screams
A Silent Moon
Pouring Silver Dreams, Down the Streets

I Set my Soul
Blood Riding Ghost
On a Riverside Bank
Stones, Running Slow Tonight

Hey, Darling Faraway!
Send me a Thought
Blow it, into Mist of Moon Clouds

And She Dreams
Selene the Moon
Diving down, Young Soul

I Set my Soul, Stone Riverside
And Drink her Spirit's Blood
With my Sailing Ghost
Stones, Running Slow Tonight

Darling Faraway
Send me a Silent Thought
Blow it into Daydream
And I Believe
It Will Rain Light Moonstones on your Side

Lady Loon's Blood
Running Closer than You Thought

Lady Long Leg Liar

It's Late July
On One of Venus' Moons
Dust Devil ... Making it's Way
On a Trail
She used to Walk Her Wild Cat
... Night and Days
Until something came
Shoot the Sweet Heart
To Sand and Spark

Autumn Wind and Rain
Leaving Footprints on Misty Hay
On a Trail
Her Hips used to Sway
On that Innocent May

O' It's a Mantis ... on her Pray
Just Light Swing of Leaf
On a still young Tree

O' Lady Long Leg
'Marching, Her Champs Elysee'
Spring, Sparkling up the Air
Someone Pouring Champagne
On Street of Flaming Roses

And Lady Long Leg
Got her Mantis on a Pray
Just Light Swing of Leaf
On Hips of still Young Tree

It's Late July ... on Venus Moon
Dust Devil, on Mars Dream, Passes Close-by
Raising its Toes and Tail, up the sky
O' My Fool Heart

22

Summer's Gone, Julianne

O' Julianne, O' Julianne
   Summer's Gone, Julianne
Fade away
   Fade Away, Julianne

"... Last days of Lover's Games ..."

O' Julian, Go Away
   Summer's Gone, Gone Away
O' Feel that Wind
   Flushing Our Cheekbones

A Single Breaking Leave
   On Early Autumn Air
Colours of Fall
   Raising French Maiden Hair
   Swing, Babe Swing, on Autumn Wind
   Summer's Gone
    Flown Away, Flown Away

Cold Sky-Blue
   Shivering Down, On Roots
   Deep into White of Bones
O' Julianne, O' Julianne
   Lover's Game, Julianne

See that Long Neck Swan
   Spreading Wings, Heaven-Wide
Dreaming Southern Sunlight

O' Julianne
   Throw Your Last Eye
   Lover's Coup D'oeil
O' Julian

Shadow Master Takes the Stage
It's Lover's Last Game

O' Julianne, O' Julianne
I May Forget Your Name
O' Julian, Julian
It's Your Last Game

Swing, Babe Swing, On Early Autumn Air
Summer's Gone
Summer's Gone, With a Wind
It's a Lover's Last Breathe

ROME FALLS

After howling the Moon and her Maidens, let us dive to a world of more serious philosophy. Title might be too dramatic for some of the lyrics, but who wants to be Caesar of the boring ones. It's a mental journey, in many ways.

Interestingly, the section Rome Falls got name from a poem written just months before world lockdown in 2020. Think about the famous saying '*All roads lead to Rome*'. Then, have a slow thought of relativity of words 'Rome' and 'Home'. Of course here, the name refers also to personal feelings, experiences and Amor.

The concept of Rome is fascinating, no doubt. After adapting and developing Greek democracy, culture and gods, Rome turned to a great empire with first unforgettable emperors. Gods in Greek mythology have inspired this work a lot – so much that I have invited some of them to join – and so have the exciting, almost unbelievable stories on history of Rome. And as we all very well know the Eternal City still stands in a fountain of time.

Now, I just let you be the Emperor of your own Little Empire ...

Vanilla Sky

O' Boy, What a Feeling
I got my own Vanilla Sky Dream

My Boy, Running on Fires of the Night
Never Settling, Young Heart's Beating

And on Morning, Unreal Date
Face Beaten
Blind Eye Zen
And Blood Running on Streets

' O' I got my own Vanilla Sky '

Say you need a Cigarette
Say you need a Doctor
And Police Force
Hey
It's just my Psyche
On a Stolen Phone

Come, Philosopher Come
See the Truth, Blind Eye Zen
O' I Got my own Vanilla Sky

Got Beaten on Streets
Beaten on Sports
Beaten on Holy Night Wars
O' Blind Eye Zen
Mirror's Broken
People Looking on Strange Ways

O' I Got my Vanilla Sky

You Know those Lessons

Life Likes to Throw
Without Asking, on your Face

O' It's a Big Buddha Smile
On your Stolen Phone
Likes to Know, How do you Like
'Blind Eye Zen'

O' I Got my own Vanilla Sky

And on Morning, Unreal Date
With Queen Narcissus
Looking your Beaten Face
There's your Blood on Streets
You've reached, Blind Eye Zen

Got your own Vanilla Sky

Remove my Role

I Will Take-off my Role
Take Off Whole Wardrobe
Remove my Status
And Hidden Arms

I Take-Off all my Cloths
And Walk Back to the Ocean Blue
Slowly, as a Fool of a Moon ... is Cool

When I Finally Rise
I Rise with Mountain Side Hills
And Sit, next to my Elephant-Wise
And Think the Way the Trees Do

As I Shiver Down the Cold Blue
And Wait for the Night Stars to Spark
My Soul Sheds an Empty Skin
On a Lonely Paradise Beach
And My Wolf Howls the Moon

Rome Falls Tonight

'What if Rome would Fall Tonight'

It's a Dangerous Game
Tree Tearing Tiger Stripes, on Skin
And She's Wild
With Hungry Eyes, for the First Time

O' Babe, Had a Dream
Rome Falling Tonight
It's a Dangerous Game
Turning Clock Around
Breathing Heart all Out

'And I Call my Nine'
Muses Firing Soul Blind
Kiss me, Calliope
I Take off my Role, Whole Wardrobe

And Call my Nine
Muses Firing Soul Blind
Nymphs Dancing, Sylvan Falling over Horizon

O' Selene
What if Time, Was just a Red Line
Flowing through your Heart's Mind

'What if Rome, would Fall Tonight'

Love, War and Philosophy
O' Babe, It's a Dangerous Game
Tree Tearing Tiger Stripes on Skin
Alligator Eyes, Shooting Stars
And She Whisper's to my Ear
There's a Road close ... Leading Nowhere

What if Rome would Fall Tonight?

O' Babe, I had a Dream
   'Rome Falling Tonight'
      Ghost Moonwalking Back in Time
         Landing into Youth Tribe

O' Babe, What if Rome Falls Tonight?

Blood Bath

My Body, Floating, on a Warm, Blood Bath
Got a Call, Not my favorite God
Can't Choose Your Parents, Dude

Floating on a Warm, Blood Bath
Got Argument, on my Lil' Senate
Of Course, I got Great A – On my Short Veins

Hey, Hear
2nd Consul's Boring Speech
All Gods Falling Asleep
So I March, with Soldiers' Drunk
On Poor Paths, Trough Unknown Worlds

My temple, and Holy Soul
Floating, on a Warm, Blood Bath
I Got my Own Civil War
Hunting Down, Cheek Opposite
Officer, and All Intellectual
Cut the Head
Break the Nose
Statue must Fall
O' Ave
Priest and Pope
Tax Decimus, on Thumb's Wave

O' My Body and Soul
Floating on a Warm, Blood Bath
Got a Call, Not my Favorite Gods
Neither Can you Choose Parents
Red White Diplomacy, Dude
Got an Argument, on my Lil' Senate Floor
Old Greek God, Spilled some Wine
On, a Toga White

Time, a Strange King

My Temple Knight
    Floating, On a Warm, Blood Bath
  On Street, On Private Club
     On a Holy Ground
    Thousand Years
       Lambs Grown Lion Teeth, on Their Back

Got a Call, Not my Favorite God
    You must Be Mad, Open your Mouth
  While, God's Pouring, Bad Wine
     On Olympos High
  Can't Choose Your Parents, Little Fool

Notre Dame Down

Eins, Zwei - Eins, Zwei, Drei
Eins, Zwei, Drei
Monsoon and Tsunami
Ice Age Avalanche

Apostles Tweeting On Streets
'Notre Dame Down
Notre Dame Down'

Hey, Lady Green
Light my Fire, Please

S'il Vous Plait
Someone Smoking White Clouds
Lingering the Streets

Virgin, Saint and Martyr
All Pointing Fire @ Your Heart

Hey Lady Green, Light my Fire, Please
'Notre Dame Down
Notre Dame Down'

Monsoon and Tsunami
Apostles Tweeting on Misty Streets
Someone Smoking, Holy Marijuana
White Clouds Slowly Lingering
... Seine Stone Floors

Hey Lady Green
Light my Fire, Please
Moonwalking Dracula, Googling Sunstare
Virgin, Martyr and Beheaded Queen
'Notre Dame Down

Notre Dame Down'

Someone Smoking Renaissance Art
White Clouds Lingering, Seine Stone Floor
Notre Dame Down, Notre Dame Down

34

Sometimes, You're a King

Sometimes, You're a King
*   Sometimes, You're just Left Alone*
* Sometimes ... A Day*
*   And then a Night*

Sometimes, You're a King
*   Sometimes, Just a Fool, Playing Around*

Sometimes, God Calls by your Name
*   Sometimes, Your Blood Burns for Love*
*   Sometimes, Winter Comes*
*   And Freezes your Heart*
Sometimes, You're a King
*   Sometimes, You Think*
*   All belong to Race of Apes*
* Sometimes*
*   Just a Forgotten Prince on Lion's Mouth*

Sometimes, It's a Day
*   Sometimes, Your Heart Burns Stones of Fate*

Sometimes
*   You're Dragged & dropped*
*   Back to Point One*
* Sometimes, Lady Roseline Dream*
*   Sends her Seasons, Running Over Me*

Sometimes, you're a King
* Sometimes, it's the Fool*
*   That Takes the Game*

Sometimes, You're a King
* Sometimes, Wind Blows*
*   Right through Your Heart*

Sometimes A Day
And then A Night
Sometimes
You Lean on North Wind's Freezing Heart

36

Loosing My Skin

Loosing my Skin
*   Been on Road too Long*
* Sleeping with Snakes*
*   Vipers, on my Bed*

Born on Ocean Dream
*   Raised by a Mountain Wind*
*   Sailing, on a Moon Wave*
I've Rained my Sins
*   Dry Skin, and Saharan Soul*

Loosing my Skin
*   Been on Road too Long*
* Sleeping with Snakes*
*   Vipers Warming my Bed*

Born on Ocean Dream
*   Raised by a Mountain Wind*
*   Rained my Sins*
* Loosing my Soul*
*   Grown too Big and Cool*
*   Taken by a Young Moon*
*   Rained my Sins*
*   Down Cactus Roots*
*   No one really knows my Name*

Loosing my Skin
*   Been on Road too Long*
* Meeting my Snake Soul*
*   Old Man, taking off Jacket Blue*
*   Smiling to Young Boy Eyes*

I'm 'Loosing my Skin
*   Loosing my Skin'*

Stone Soul Statue

Lost my Breath
    Lost Air, under my Wings
    Landed Down, on Autumn Tree Leaves

Soul Feels Heavy like a Stone
    Strings Drawing my Veins Down Red Ground
      Guess Someone Bigger
        Trying to Tell me a Tale, or End One

Settling here for Awhile
    Hope You Feel It Too
      Season Changing Mood

Wind Carving a Stone Statue
    Soul Slows Seconds to Years
      Welcome Ghost to White Marble House
Takes 2 Thousand Years to empty this Chalice

Lost my Breath
    Air under my Wings
      Landed Down on Autumn Leaves

Soul's a Heavy Stone
    Draws Veins Down to Ground
    Big Fellow Taking a Time-Out
    Hope You Feel It Too

Wind Carving Statue out of Stone
    Soul Taking Pose
      On Garden of White Marble House
Selene, Waiting for a Full Blood Moon Rise
    Takes Few Thousand Years
      Refill my Chalice, Silver Shadows of You

Try & Fail

You Try, and You Fail
You Aim, and Rise Expectations
You Prepare, and Make Your Way

Just to Notice
The Door, Closed for Now
You Breathe, and Swear Gods
They Should Know

You Reach Your Knees
Seek Something to Stand On
Dim Light of Hope, from Distant Horizon

But No One's There
All Alone in the Darkness

You Seek Something to Try on
Weak Hearted God's Soft Moment
Last Liana, on Lion Yard

You Try, and You Fail
You Prepare, and Aim Higher
Take Your Shot

Just to Notice
It Was Nothing, But a Dead Man's Breath

Gone With A Wind

Knock Knock, Anyone There
Knock, Knock, Knock
Been Knocking an Empty Chest
Earth's Hollow Crust

Tell your Mom
Tell your Friends
You're Gone ... Gone with a Wind
Swallowed by the Earth

Tell your Mom
Your Neighborhood
Tell it, To a Young Mountain Moon
To a Distant Monsoon
Seeking its Way, on Ocean Wide
Tell You're Gone ...Gone with a Wind

Fate, a Strange Game
For a Soul, Sailing Seven Seas
Ok Slow now
Walking on Street of Thinking Trees
On a River-Bed Rocks Speak

Tell your Mom
Tell your Childhood Friend
Tell it, to your First Love
You're Gone, Taken by Time
Swept Away, by High-Blood Tide

O' Fires of the World
Tell your Mom
Tell, to a Winding Tree
Tell it, to First Snow, of North
You're Gone
Sailed away, Thousand Moon Waves

Tell your Mom, Tell your Friends
Tell Your Summer Love
Write a Letter, to your Graveyard
Tell it to an Ocean Wave
Looking for a Paradise Apple Tree
Remember me, from my Eyes of the World

You're Gone, Gone with a Wind
With a by-walking Cloud
Sailed Away, an Ocean Dream

ATLANTIS SOUL

'*Atlantis*', I just lost my breath, for a century – maybe my mental Titan-ic is sinking.

The myth tells that there's great wisdom, richness and an advanced city lost somewhere in the, most likely, Atlantic Ocean. If you have a more realistic personality, you may think that Atlantic Ocean is so huge and wide that it has not been a problem to loose a city, or two, on its shores before '*we got airborne*'.

Well, they say that Atlantic Ocean got name from Titan Atlas, hero of Greek mythology. He was doomed to hold the heaven up on his shoulders for the rest of his life. For someone like him, there's a little Titan lullaby:

> *Once upon the time*
> *A Man Hold up the Sky*
> *With his Arms above his Head*
> *But the Time came, and past*
> *And he got old and tired*
> *Now, He was holding up the Heavens*
> *With hands just above shoulders*
> *So, he was with his new friends ... Stars, and a Moon*

Have you found, are you aware of, your Soul? Or is it lost like Atlantis?

Whisper in a Wind

A Whisper in a Wind
   On a Distant Ocean Wave
      She's Calling on Her Way

O' My Darling Wide-Eye
   Fool's Dream ... on a Fairy Tale

Cut Your Roots
   And Light that Torch
      We Are Going to Burn, some Old Soul
         You, Me and Gandalf the Gray

Zensei Air

Hey Sensei!
  Can You Feel?
    Atlantic Breeze
  Can You Hear?
    Blue Sky Call

Scent of a Sun
  Bird Senses
    Wide-Sky-Eye
  Thought of God

Hey Zensei! Takeoff
  Hold your Breathe, Here We Go

Remember Who You Are
  Rain, River and Ocean-Heart
    Wind and Free Air
  Saint One, Burning Bird Soul

Hey Fly-Master, Sailing Ocean Air
  Can You Feel the Beat?
    Blue Blood, Riding Waves on Ocean A

Hey Zensei Air
  It's a Dream
    God's Whisper
      On Blue Cloud Street

Say 'Zen'
  Pure Life, Pura La Vida
    Spirit Yoga on Air
  Bird Senses
    Scent of a Sun
      Castles of Clouds

Flying Heart
    It's a Dream, God's Whisper
        Soul Wind, Shivering Ancient Grounds

Hey Zensei, Wide-Sky-Eye
    Can You Feel, Atlantic Breeze
        Scent of a Sun, Spirit of Bird

    Rain, River and Ocean-Heart
        Wind and Free Air
    Saint One, Burning Bird Soul

Lone Survivor

Hey Lone Survivor
    Sold your Soul?
Blue Devil's Smile
    Sailing it on Ocean Wide

Had Your Close Call
    Shadow, Touched your Little Faint Heart
Hey Captain
    Sold your Soul, to all Pirate's Wife
Run, You Hollow Fool
    Pissed-off Guardian Angel too

Hey Lady Strange, Please
    Having, Violent Dreams
Sold my Soul
    Dust to Diamonds of Moon
Pour me, Café de Mortale
    I'll be Smoking, Devil's Cigarette

So, you had your Close Call
    Shadow of Mars, Dialing your Phone
O' Bella Mar, Sold my Soul
    Dust, to Diamonds circling Moon

Hey, Lady Strange
    Having unpleasant Dreams
Pour me, an Ocean of Hope
    From Pandora's Jar
I'll be Smoking, on Devil's Table
    Don't tell anyone, if no Angel in Heart

Hey, Lady Strange
    Light a Candle, Please
    Hope, for my Cold Night

Have you Seen, my poor Ghost
Sailing on these Seas
You know what they say
Cursed Love
Devil's Last Wish
Sell a Soul, for a Highest Bid

Can you See, Hear?
Dust of Moon, Raining Down
Soul, of a Survivor
Ruins, of Atlantis

Hey Lone Survivor, it's an Ocean Wide

Flamboyant

My Soul's a Tree
  On a Seaside Cliff
And I Feel Fresh Green
    On Music Bar Avenue
    Burning my Torch of Freedom
        On Raised Hand of a Little God

Cross-Stretch my Arms
      Branch for a Bird, Flying-by
And I Drop a Dream of You
      Leaf, into Flirting Air
      Feeling Flamboyant, Flamboyant

Circled Moon or Two
    Since last Rain Clouds Passed-by
But have my Roots
      Still on Something Moist and Wet

Solitude and Serenity
    National Geography Photo-Shoot
Dude
      Mermaids Waving Tails on Dry Lands

Feeling Flamboyant
    O' my Favorite Dog
        Lifting Leg, High on my Roots

My Soul's a Tree
      On a Seaside Cliff
Swinging my Leaves
      On Early Eve's Breeze

Solitude and Serenity
    African Plain Mountain Peak

All the Rock Stars that won't Speak

My Soul's a Tree
On Seaside Cliff
And I Drop a Dream
Leaf, a Memory of You, Inside Out
Shadow of a Moon Soul

'Feeling Flamboyant, Flamboyant'

Silhouette on Sky

Silhouette on Sky

Someone's Having Dreams
Sailing on my Thoughts
Need a Table, for my World
Clear Out, Motion of Clouds

Silhouette on Sky
Someone Having a Dream

Devil, Dressed on Barista Code
She's Pouring Little Sins
Into Ocean of Souls

Filtering, Last Rain
Through the Street Leaves
My Ghost
Just Got Lost
On Highlands of Caffeine

Filtering, My Soul
Catching Dreams Wind Blows

Silhouette on Sky
Someone Having Strange Thoughts

And I Hear a Mermaid's Voice
Desire of Ocean
Joy of its Waves
Why Don't You, Soul Dive
On Tonight's Moon Tide?

And I have my Paradise Déjà Vu
'Devil's Pouring Little Sins

Into Ocean of Souls'

And I Feel Someone's Dreams
Sailing on my Thoughts

'Silhouette on Sky, Silhouette on Sky'

Atlantis Sign

My Mom Says, I'm Cuban Slim
And My Pa, I Should Find a Girl
Who's not Smoking
While Driving Alone
Dam Sunny Coastline
And My Friends, Some Grown Old
Some Think they Know it All

Hi Captain!
Got your Cigarettes?
Had my Double Espressos
An Ocean of Americano
Tell Me, Please
If You See a Shore, Il Capitano

Walking Streets
In a Town They Call, Little Atlantis
And someone told
Noah still on Ark

And I Throw a Silver Dime
From a Treasure I Found
To every Corner
To Find my Way Back Home
On a Some Poor Day
And I am Having a Caribbean Dream
Dimes Tingling, on Pockets bigger than Shorts
Had my Espressos
And now River Red
Opens to an Ocean of Americano

And Hey Captain, Tell me
If you See a Shore, Il Capitano
Sitting on a Chest

Hidden in a middle of Park, Called Noah Ark

I Throw a Dime
Silver Above a Table Round
And If I had Wings, I would Fly

My Mom Says, I'm Cuban Slim
My Dad, Thinks Havana is on Moon
And some, they are Kings of the World

And I ... Having a Caribbean Dream
'Throwing a Dime, Silver on Atlantis Sign'
They Say, Noah still on Ark
And I Dive, into a Double Espresso
Sesam, Door Dark and Gold
It's an Ocean of Soul

Inner Island

My Soul's a View on Ocean Wide
Where I'm Building a Temple High
My Heart ... is an Island Tide

Found my Old, Found my Youth
Found my Hideaway
Grew my Soul Tree
Talked to my Guardian Angel

Built my Temple Slow
Buddhist Stone Statue
Spread some Chakra, on Lotus Pose
Got Even, with my Inner Island

Got Even, With my Inner Island
Found my Old, Found my Youth
Found my Hideaway Escape
Grew my Soul Tree
Talked to my Guardian Bird

Built my Temple Slow
Buddhist Stone Statue
Spread Seven Chakra
On Field of Lotus Rose

Got my Things Done
Balanced my Soul
Got Even
With my Inner Island

And Now I Feel Tropical Green
... Nordic Chill
Found my African Twin
... French Speaking

O' my Latin Heart
... Temper Roman Smart

Found my Inner Peace
Got Even, with Sins of Past

My Soul's a View on Ocean Wide
Where I'm Building a Temple High

'My Heart, is an Island Tide '

Somewhere in Time

Somewhere in Time
      Thousand Roses Cry
  Somewhere in Time
         Tomorrow's Fools
             Dancing Young Moon Down

O' King of Africa
      How do you Smile?
  Somewhere in Time
         Tomorrow's Fools
              Playing with Heart's High-Tide
  Trying to Change, Lady Nature's Mind

O' Queen of Africa
     Somewhere in Time
         Young Fool Rides

O' Somewhere in Time
     Thousand Steps Down, Rising Moon
          'Roses Cry'

O' Somewhere in Time
      There's a Smile, Shooting Mirror Eye-Glide
          Changing Lady Nature's Mind
                 'Lady Nature's Mind'

O' King of Africa
      How Wide do you Smile?
  Somewhere in Time
         Tomorrow's Fools
             Dancing Down Young Moon

Thousand Steps Down
      On a Planet Dark and Blue

Queen of Heart, Princess Africa
Walks on Field, Roses Cry
'Roses Cry'

Somewhere in Time
Tomorrow's Fools
Weighing up the Moon

Soul Shadow

It was Born on Ocean Dream
Raised, by a Mountain Wind
Clouds and Bird Thoughts
Songs of the Woods

Like a Soul Shadow
Stalking Me
Wonder does it Dream
Sixty Shades, of Summer Eves
Sixty Shades of Summer Eves

Like a Soul Shadow
Searching Light, on Eternal Path
And you Never Know
How Does It Feel
When Your Soul, Blind Card Deals

Like a Soul Shadow
Walking Down a Street
Wonder does it Dream?
Sixty Shades, of Moon Tides

Babe, I think
It was Born on Ocean Dream
Raised by a Mountain Wind
Clouds and Birds
Songs of Wild

Like a Soul Shadow
Searching Youth
I Wonder Does It Ever Figure Out
Its Meaning, All-given Roles

Like a Soul Shadow

Stalking in my Dreams
I Wonder does it Feel Desire, Endless Need
Sixty Shades, of Summer Eve
Sixty Shades of Summer Eve

Babe, I Think
It Was Born, on Ocean Wind
Raised, by a Mountain Wind
Clouds and Bird Thoughts
Songs of Woods and Wild

Liquid Sex

You Say, You're Smooth
You Say, You're a Jungle Cat
With Every Move
And They Say
You're a Social Snake, in a Botanical Garden
Spider, in a World Wide Web

O' You're Smooth
Poison Diamonds, Dracula Tooth
Smooth, Liquid Skin
Wind Speech

O' a Lonely Boat, Sailing on a Dance Floor

And They Say
It's just a Dream
Something Never Been

O' She's Smooth, Jungle Cat
Liquid, Doped Romantic
Got Melting Ice Cubes
Fresh Breath, Wind Speed
O' She's Pure Soul, Hiding Dangerous Beast

It's Just a Dream
Something Blue, Never Been
And the Wave
Born on Ocean Soul, Star Breeze
She's a Lonely Boat, On a Blue Dancing Floor

And They Say, She's just a Dream
Something Blue, Never Been
Salty Tear of Pirate Fear

She's Super-Smooth, Blood Diamonds on Dracula Tooth

And the Blue Ocean Wave, Cheating my Fate

61

Carping Diem

Wake-up Darling Dollar-Eye
Six Senses Carping Diem
Life Surfacing Time

Four Elements, All God Damn Alchemists
Throwing Dreams
Heart Beats of Emotions

O' Lady Blue Lagoon Moon
Sixty Shades of Devil's Glow

Deep Breathe
Sixty Seconds Dive
Into Ocean of Emotions
Hate, Anger, Love
Venus, Doing it with Mars
Raining Sadness, In a Sea of Joy

Wake-up Darling Dollar-Eye
Yin and Yang Go Blind
Six Senses Carping Diem
Four Elements, All God Damn Alchemists
Throwing Dreams, Heart Beats of Emotions
Into your Gra-Vital Turn

O' Lady Blue
Waking Sixty Shades of Moon
Leonardo Da Cupido, Shooting Down Stars
Lullaby, Old Gods

Deep Breathe
60 Seconds Dive, Into Ocean of Emotions
Wake-up, Darling Desire
Hate, Anger and Love

All, Doing it with Venus and Mars

O' Lady Ocean Blue
Soul Yin and Yang, Surfing Queen Desire
Six Senses Carping Diem
4 Elements, All God Damn Alchemists
Throwing Devil's Lost Dreams
Heart Beats of Emotions, into Air
It's Raining Sadness, In Seven Seas of Joy

Wake-up Darling Dollar Eye
Six Senses Carping Diem

Havana-Cubana

Hey, Columbus
   It is Cuba, Libre for All
     Share it with the Crew
  Cigarettes for All

Hey, Captain
   Can't make a mistake
     Those Shores We Know
  See, how Spirit Grows

It's Time for a Cuban
   Cut a head
     From a Cigarette
  Moist the Lips
    Gonna Light It Up
     Fire of Earth, Swing on Salsa Hips

Feel the Power, Il Capitano
   Ship's Flying
     Even Helmsman Rowing

See, the Palm Tree Bending
   On Atlantic Breeze

Cuban Deep Breathe
   Feel the Caribbean Sun
    Burning Sailor Skin

Breathe Babe, Breathe
   Breathe Caribbean Island Deep
  Till Your Eyes Catch Bonfires
    On Cuban Beach Nights

LADY EA

Welcome, *Renaissance of Heart!* Let '*my little Apollo*' do the well-deserved introduction, he is a sort of professional on this field, anyways:

Heart's Rose

I Bow my Heart's Rose
After Moon Maiden's Smile
May it Fly, Butterflies
On Your Soul's Way
Raise its Winds, Mountain Highs
Let your Spring
Play White and Green
Run Summer Sun down the Hills

Lady Ea

She's Wild, She's Myth
She's Inviting, and Exciting
Yet, Safe and Sound
On a Dangerous Ground
She's Mistress ... Wild Heart

Since Day One

I've Been Here
Since Day One
Been Here, Since Day One

And Nothing Feels Like, You Coming By
Nothing Feels Like, Stars Collide

Been Here, Since Day One
Since Day One
Been a Road to Run
Seen you Growing, Slowly Dying

And Now, Back to Point One
Beyond Moons Julian
Searching for a Different Light
Different Mood
Sitting Down, Next to my Elephant Wise
Viewing Side Trails
Just for a Change

In my Dreams
Walking Red River Nile
Down to South, Back in Time
Where Soul has Nothing to Hide
Feel that Familiar Sight
Staring Back at Grass Line
Lion Measuring Blood's Pride

And Below Skin
Something's Moving like a Snake
Paradise Hidden
Walking now with my Elephant-Wise
It's a Beautiful African Wide

I've Been Here Since Day One
Since Day One

And Nothing Feels like you Coming By
Big Bang! Stars Collide
Feels like Day One
'... Day One ...'

Bring Me Tomorrow

Hey, Darling Dream-Eye
Moonlight Desire

Bring Me Tomorrow
Bring Me, Tomorrow's Shadow

Crystal Ball, and Swirling Skies
There's Magic, on Your Moves

'Bring Me Tomorrow'

O' Darling Dream-Eye
Light of Shooting Stars
Pour It, into my Glass
Streams, of Seven Seas
Glazier, and Desert
For those who can not See

Bring Me Tomorrow
Dream its Shadows
Light of Evening Stars
Pour it into my Glass

'... Moonlight Desire ...'

Hey Darling Dream-Eye
Magic on Your Moves
Swirling Skies

Bring Me Tomorrow
Dream its Shadows
Light of the Shooting Stars
Pour it, into my Glass
Rain, Rain of Time

'Rain of Time'

Darling Dream-Eye
Moonlight Desire
Bring Me Tomorrow
Bring Me Tomorrow's Shadow

Raining Sugar

Maybe One Day
   Devil Wounded God
      And a Drop of Blood
         Stoned Blue on Courtyard
Maybe One Day
   They'll Call It, Something like Love

And Now, She's Walking Her Ghost
   On Borderline of my Soul
I Guess, Venus Blowing Her Winds
   Into Flames of Desire

And After All
   It's Raining Sugar
      On my Cup of Coffee
Small Magic Drums
   Waking Mountain Zen
   So the Souls Collide
      Rising a Faint Moon Smile
        Only Clouds Can Hide

I Guess, There Was a Storm
   Somewhere in Paradise

And Now, It's Raining
      Sugar on my Coffee
Venus Blowing Her Sweet Winds
   On Ocean of Souls

And She's Walking Her Ghost
   On Borderline of my Soul
Small Witch Drums
   Talking to my Mountain Zen

O' Spirit Freeze
    Baby-Steps to Future, Please
  And a Rain of Stars
      Rolling Over Cool Nights Past
  Sleep-Walking my Zen
      Hunting Her Ghost Down
        On Mountain Clouds

And I Know, On Morning
  It's Raining Sugar
    On my Cup of Coffee

Walking Her Cats

On a Dreamy Day's Wave
*   Diana Searching Her Soul's Mate*
* She's Walking Her Cats*
*   Down Castles on Natural Gardens*

And a Demi-Lune Weighs
*   Pink and White*

All the Owls of the Woods
*   Shall be Beheaded by their Looks*
* As Lady of the Hunt*
*   Lingers through the Wilds*

Between Emotion and Thought
*   I Finally Get a Call*
* All Secretaries with their Wings Wide*
*   Tell it's a God, and has a Great Plan*

And a Fierce Sound of a Wind
*   Carves Marks on my Bones*
* Early Earth's Spell*
*   Casted over my Soul*

Between Moon and Mood
*   I Hear You Whisper*
*   In Language of a Night and Day*

She's Walking her Wild Cats
*   All Ten-and-One*
*   Deep Through the Natural Parks*
* And a Demi-Lune Weighs, All Pink and White*

From Shadows of Leaves
*   And Cracks of Dinosaur Bones*

I Hear her Cats Silent Roar
She's Walking her Mistresses, All Ten and One
Demi-Lune Weighs, all Pink and White

And She's Walking
Hundred-and-One, Dalmatians on a Light Hunt
Between Memory and Starry Night
I Hear her Cats Distant Roar

She's Walking Her Wild Cats
On Dreams of Thousand-and-One

O' Life

O' Life
>*All the Things, You Make Me Do*
O' Life
>*All the Feelings, You Share*

O' Life
>*All the Choices*
>>*You Force Me to Take*
All the Mountains
>*You Make Me Climb*
O' Life, All the Blood
>*Your Heart Drinks, Today*

O' Life
>*Sweet Curse*
>>*Hunting a Sour Purpose*

O' Life
>*All the Love You Bleed*
>>*All the Girls you Make me Fall*
>>>*And All the Love You Take Away*
It's an Ocean of Blood
>*Since Day One*

O' Life
>*All the Fool Things*
>>*You Make Me Believe*
All the Stories
>*Your Crazy Mind Tells in a Day*
>*O' It's a New Day*
>>*Choices on your Hands*
>>>*All the Cards of Fate*

O' Life

All the Things You Create
    All the Miracles, Your Wild Feels
Feel, You're Alive
    All the Green, Thrown up the Sky
O' Life
      All the Wings, You Grow
        All the Snow, Your Angels Blow

O' Life
    All the Things, You Make Me Dream
    All the Secrets You Hold
      All the Surprises, You Share

Leather Bronze Suit

*I Miss my Mediterranean Philosophy
   Endless Cliff Trails, Olive Tree Shades*

*Would Love to Walk
   On that Road, Leading Nowhere
I Miss my Leather Bronze Suit
   Worn Sandals, Yesterday's Wine Bottle Smile*

*I Miss my Leather Bronze Suit
   Long Day on a Sunny Bay
Would Love to Chase Aphrodite
   Hiding in Small-Tight Bikini*

*I Miss my Meditative Thoughts
   Chatting with Ocean Blue*

*Would Love to See you Sleeping
   On a Chair Café La Terasse
Kissing Dionysus's Mistress
   On a Tropical Day-Dream*

*Would Love to Wear
   My Leather Half-God Bronze Suit Again
Chase Aphrodite, Hiding under Tight Bikini*

*I Miss my Palm Tree Tall
   I Miss my Meditative Thoughts
   Chatting with Ocean Blue*

*Would Love to Walk, Road Leading Nowhere
   Pull Behind Superman's Cloak
   Sewn on Thousand and One Dream*

I Miss my Leather Bronze Suit

Timeworn Roman Sandals
And Yesterday's Wine Bottle Smile
Would Love to Chase Aphrodite
Hiding under Tight Bikini

'Chasing Aphrodite, Chasing Aphrodite'

I Miss my Meditative Line of Horizon
Love to See, a Mediterranean Leaf
Flying over Road, Leading Nowhere

'Cause you might already be there'

Tour de Gongo

O' What a Day
And I Asked my Bicycle
Out for a Date
And She Just Said

'Tour de Gongo ... Tour de Zaire'
And a Summer Wind Hails
Cheeks, Bones, Yesterday's Pains
Breaks, Statue Chains

Took a Bicycle Out for a Date
Sun on my Skin
Shadows of Leaves
Bird's Final Glide, from a Migration Flight

And on Light Summer Wind
She Just Said

'Tour de Gongo, Tour de Zaire'

Le Petit Monde
Let it Roll, Let it Shine
Tour de Gongo, Tour de Zaire

Rainforest Running Down Equator Line
And a Summer Wind Prays
Mist out of Mountain Shades

O' What a Day

And I Took a Bike
Out for a Date
And She just Says

'Tour de Gongo, Tour de Zaire'

And all the Butterflies
    Playing in a Paradise
  Like Monarchs, born on Milkweed Leaves
      Rising on Autumn Air
    And a Summer Wind Hails
        Breaks Long Winter, on Statue Chains

'Tour de Gongo, Tour de Zaire'

Libre La France

Eins, Zwei; Eins, Zwei; Eins, Zwei, Drei
Monsoon and Tsunami
Lady Green, Dancing on a Hurricane

Libre La France
Libre La France
Libre La France

Old Country
Old Customs
Old Moves
Vineyards, as Far as Eye can Fly

O' Lady Green
Say Hello to Queen
Marie Antoinette, Louis Sun King
All the Castles
Tree Colours
And Road to Versailles
Hear the Wind, of Fading Renaissance

Say it Loud
Say it Soft

Libre La France
Libre La France
Libre La France

Old Nation
Old Blood
Spring Blooming on Vineyards
Spill your Heart
Spill Your Heart

O' Lady Green, Au Revoir
    'Fading Renaissance, Fading Renaissance ...'

81

Moon's on Fire

On a First Breathe of Spring
    Summer Eves' Shadows Fall
Diana, Howls Hunter's Moon
    Down, Back to Earth
    Waking-up Old Mountain God

O' You, Green Pretty Little Thing
    Bring Me Down, My Temple High
Moon's on Fire, Tonight

Maybe She's Still Dreaming, Dragon Screams
    Hiding, Last Egg of a Dinosaur

O' Lady of a Four Sea
    Seven States of Moon, Changing Phase
        Storm Rising, on your Heels
O' You, Who Shadows all the Green
        Lady Fate has Strange Dance Moves
You Know How it Feels?
        Goddess, Rising Young Blood

'Moon's on Fire Tonight'

She is Wild, She is Myth
    She's Inviting, She's Exciting
She's Mistress Earth, Theater of Moods

O' Lady, Tiding Young Men's Hearts
    Moon's on Fire Tonight

On a Rise of Mountain God
    Diana Howls Down a Blue Star
O' You Green Pretty Little Thing
    Bring me Down, My Temple High

'Moon's on Fire, Tonight'

If I Only Wear You

If I Were You
> *Had Eyes on that Mood*
> *If I only Were You*

Everyone Feels
> *She's a Natural Force*
> *Eyes, of the World*
> *Size, of a Moon*

If I only Wear You
> *Chill of the Night, Light of a Day*
> *If I only Wear You*
> *Eyes, size of a Moon*
> *Soul, Burning Fires of Earth*

Everyone Sees
> *She's a Natural Force*
> *Walking her own Mountain Peaks*
> *Even on Crowds*
> *Has Her Own Circling Crown of Crows*

If I only Wear You
> *Zodiacs of the Night*
> *Falling Shadows of Time*

'If I only Wear You'

And on a Boring Day
> *All Rain and Gray*
> *Feel your Spirit growing Light*
> *Soul and Source of Life*

And on Your Waning Eyes
> *My Dreams Dive*

'If I only Wear You, If I Only Wear You'

SUMMER CITY SUN

So hot, it got to be summer. No need to explain, but some chosen lines with good summer moods should serve you the idea what this chapter is about:

A Fresh Breath of Wind – Scent of a Sun – It's Raining Slow Time – Feel That Old Ocean Beat – Wind Blowing, When Venus Walks By – Let my Lover Cute, Steal Your Eyes ... and Heart – O' Lady Green, Cool African Vibes – Light Your Arrows, On Cupido's Fire – Waves Falling, On Shores of Heart

Indian Summer Sky

Summer, City, Sun
   Broken Blue Jeans
      Girls Gone Wild
  Open-Heart Dreams
     Walking on Endless Streets
   Bird Wide Eyes
    Side by Flies
      Soul of a Child

'Summer Really Never Ends'

Indian Summer Sky
  Falling Out Tonight
 Strange City Vibes
   Running Down, Sun Shades
 Into City Walls
    Summer Knight's Bones Fall

Getting that Caffeine-High
  Winter Ice, on Glasses Guys
Deco and Art
  Short Summer Dresses, Gone Really Smart

Babes, Music Grooves
  Small Dancing Shoes
    Wild African Jungle Moves

O' Young Blood Riding
  Sins of Summer Sky
 And You Know the Feeling
  Soul Burning, Ancient Star Light

They Will Carve Stone Angel Chics
  Wearing Our Moves

On the City Roofs

Indian Summer Sky
Falling Out Tonight
Heart Wide
Side by Flies
Soul of a Sun

Weird Thing

Hey, It's A Weird Thing
Falling Back
Into a Memory
It's a Weird Thing
Moon Time
Stopping by Your Soul Tree

It's a Weird Feeling
High Tide
Rising on your Heart
It's Strange Thing
Sensing
Selene's Little Game Begin

O' Lady Déjà-vu
It's a Weird Feeling
When You Say 'Hi'
To a Wrong Guy

It's a Weird Thing
Being on Mood, at Wrong Time

O' Lady Déjà-vu
It's a Strange Feeling
Wind Blowing
When Venus Walks By

It's A Weird Thing
Falling Back, into a Lady Déjà-vu
It's a Strange Feeling
World, Doing the Same Spin
A Second Time

Hey, It's A Weird Feeling

Muse, Finally Taking your Hitchhike
It's a Weird Thing
> *Expectations Suddenly Colliding*

O' Lady Déjà-vu, It's a Weird Feeling
> *Heart Flooding*
>> *Falling on Selene's Little Game*

O' Lady Déjà-vu, It's A Strange Thing
> *Seeing everyone having Two Face Time*

Good Morning Vibes

Good Morning Vibes
It's Raining Slow Time
Diamonds Drumming
House of Mind

O' Smooth and Fine
Good Morning Vibe
Feels Like
Humanity Riding, Castle Time

Good Morning Vibes
Heart Beating, Cosmic Waves
Good Morning Vibes

Say Hello World
Seven Oceans, Dwelling
On your Heart

O' Good Morning Vibes
El Nino
Doing Seven Year Dives

O' Queen Marvel Eye
Orange Country All Green
Have your Slow Mo Second
Talk to Me Sky
It's Going to Be Caffeine High
God Cloud-Smoking, Good Peace Pipe

Good Morning Vibes
Good Morning Vibes

Hey Lady, Dancing Slow Time
Send Me

Good Morning Vibes
Raining Diamonds, on House of Mind

Lady Strange Weather

O' Miss Strange Weather
Storm, Rising Early Clouds
Bird Senses, Flying on Dog Hounds

Hey Babe Bird Thought
Walking on Rainmaker's Lands
Hey Lady Strange
Wind Changing Destiny
O', I can Feel It
Deep in my old Bones

O' Lady Strange
Tell Me, Who You Are
Rain, River, and Ocean Heart

Dear Destiny
Miss Strange Weather, Rising Moon
Free Air of the World, Dancing
On Rainmaker's Lands
On Rainmaker's Soul

Oh' Babe Bird Sense
Walking on Wolf Hounds
Oh' I feel it, Far from Distance
She's Riding on Ocean Breeze
And I know
Strange Weather Rising Soon

O' Lady Strange
It's Going to Rain soon
Like a Monsoon
Feel it, in my Rolling Bones

Lady Strange Weather

Burn Your Soul
        Open your Ocean Heart
Bird Senses, and Dog Hounds
        Sailing on your Season Moods
It's Going to Rain
        Rain Small Stars Tonight

Thief of Hearts

I've Been Looking for You Sometime
Asked Opinion of my Friend

Babe, I Will Steal Your Eyes
I Will Steal Your Sight
Glance by Glance
I Will Open Route to Your Heart

Babe, It Begins with just One Thought
One Mood You Share
A Feeling You Wear
I'll Steal, a Piece of Your Soul

Have a Friend
Small-One They Say
Name's Cupido
It's not Fair, I Know
He Has a Magic Bow

Babe, Sorry – Just a Thief of Hearts
Just a Thief of Hearts, I am
Piece-by-Piece, I Borrow Your Soul
Glance-by-Glance
Make my Way to your Dream World

Just One Word
Just One Face, You Share
One Mood You Wear

Babe, I Will Steal Your Heart
I Will Steal Your Love
Carry it to my Home

Just One Question, One Open Moment

And I Send my Little Friend
Shoot your Innocent Heart
Cupido to Pick Pink Roses
On your Aphrodite's Yards

Babe, So Sorry
Just a Thief of Hearts
Just a Tiny Thief, of Flying Hearts, I am

I Let my Lover Cute, Steal Your Eyes
Steal Your Sight, Dreams and Love
Just one Thought, One Mood You Share
Feeling You Wear

Yoga in a Bikini

Hey Babe, Peace
　　Yoga in a Bikini

You know the Sound
　　Wave Diving Ground
　And Feeling Inside
　　　As Big Blue Inhales
　　Let the Air Fill Your Soul
　　　It's a Mental Flow

Yoga in a Bikini, Yoga in a Bikini

Mountain and a Tree
　　Sun Rise, Bending over Pyramid Free
　　　Yoga in a Bikini
　Bow and Bridge
　　　Earth, to Sky
　Swing, Hold and Sway
　　　It's a Natural Pray

Yoga in a Bikini
　　Swing, Hold and Sway
　　　It is a Natural Pray
Say High Hi
　　Soldier of Sun
　　　　Fire Carrying Souls Tomorrow
And Wait, Distant Wave of Yesterday

Hey Babe, Peace
　　Go Low, and Ease
　See the Curves of Bay
　　　And Say 'Cheese', Yoga in Bikini
　　Cats and Dogs, Stretching Legs

Sea Breeze, Stretching Slowly Soul Wood
  Just Sand And Sea, Eyes of the World You Are

Breathe, Breathe Deep
    Move the Sun, Side to Side
      Smooth as Tide
    Triangle, Opens to Half Moon Sky
      As Day Passes By

Hey Babe Peace, Yoga in a Bikini
    Swing, Hold and Sway
  It is a Natural Pray

Lady Green

One, Two; Eins, Zwei; Uno, Dos, Tres
  Can You Feel That
          Cape Town High
    Monsoon and Tsunami
            Tiding By
      Pacific Islands
        Sinking
            Into the Big Blue Smile

O' Lady Green
    Dancing Wild
        On Mount Hurricane's Eye
  Light My Fire, Please
      Sailing to Future on your Soul Breeze

Hey, Mistress Moonshine
    Do You Feel the Same?
      El Nino, Surfing Soon

O' Eiffel High
    Curving some Time
        Tongue of Einstein
            On all Three-Stripes Tribes
Smooth African Vibes
    Leopard Heart Smiles

O' My Little Fool
    Feel That Tibet Cool
        Stars Climbing, Next to You

O' Lady Green
    Burn Your Torch Free
  O' Lady Green, Dance With Me
      O' Lady Green, Rain on Me

Rain Your Star Wise
Rain Your Jungle Might

O' Lady Green
Cool African Vibes
Eiffel, on Air Tonight
Smooth as Caribbean Hurricane Eye
Monsoon and Tsunami, Tiding By

O' Lady Green
Curving some Time tonight
Stars Climbing Next You

Cupido's Bonfire

Hey Sweet Dream
  Miss Sweet Dream
  Sensing Wild Cat Whisper
    Surrounding Innocent Beast

O' Lady Fur
  I Throw, My Lover Cute
    Into Mystery of Your Soul
And Blow an Eye Brow Breeze
  On Your Palm Tree Leaves

Hey Miss Cold Heart Sweet Dream
  Cold Heart Sweet Dream
  Sensing Basic Instincts
    Sensing Tiger Claws

And I Call, My Army of Lovers
  Light Your Arrows, Please
    On Cupido's Fire
  Hey Miss Cold Heart Sweet Dream
    Wanna See Your Soul Burn Again
      Burn on Cupido's Bonfire
        Burn on Cupido's Bonfire

O' Lady Sharp Claw
  Sending My Lover Cute
    Dancing with Mistress Fur
      Hidden in your Soul Storm

And Bowmen, Please
  Hear that Dragon-Riders Silent Scream
    Light That Fire
      Cupido's Bonfire

Thousand Dreams

O' Darling Dream
*   O' Darling Dream*
* Feel, that Deep Beat*
*   Waves Falling*
*   On Shores of Heart*

Thousand Dreams
*   Thousand Dreams*

O' Those Thousand Dreams
*   Hope Flies*
*   Moon, and Back to Earth Again*
* And All the Rain*
*   God makes, Our Stars Cry*
*   Only Angels Know*

O' Darling Dream
*   O' Darling Dream*

What if Time
*   Was a Line, Red River Growing*
*   Through Our Heart's Mind*

O' Darling Dream
*   Dream Deep*
* Feel That Old Ocean Beat*
*   Your Soul Trying to Fly, Thousand Dreams*
*   Spread Your Wings on Tomorrow's Heart Sky*

O' Darling Dream
*   Dream Deep*
*   Feel That Ocean Beat*
* Waves Falling*

On Shores of Heart

Star Knight, Searching Fallen Heart
Flying Dark, After Soul Shine Path

O' Darling Dream
Darling Dream, Dream Deep
Thousand Times
Till We Meet Again
Till We Meet Again

Saint Seventeen

Put on Your Shoes
    Best Game, and Robot Smile
    Aphrodite, Landing on Venue Mars

O' Bella, Sweet n' Sour Heart
    Arrives with a Summer Night
        Here Comes, Love in Disguise

O' Goddess Cool Down
    Saint Seventeen
        Sending Mermaid Smiles

O' Boy, Hold your Sea-Horses Down
    There She Comes
        Riding Summer Night

Pure Love, in Disguise

Say it Soft
    Say it Loud
    O' Bella, Throw me a Dice
            Throw it Twice
    Look me, with my own Eyes

O' Goddess Cool Down
    Saint Seventeen, Sending eM-eS-Gee
        Moon Waves and Mermaid Smiles

Put on Your Shoes
    Best Game, and Robot Smile
        Aphrodite Landing on Mars
    Here Comes, Love in Disguise

Hunting Barista Dream

Hear that Rhythm
Relaxed Feeling
'Hunting, Barista Dreaming'

Hunting Barista Dreaming
Mocca Clouds, Eternal Sunshine
Espresso High Tide
Surfing, on Blood Moon Light

Call that Rock Star Chill
Hollywood Smooth
'Hunting Barista Dream'

Found that High Tide
Beat, on Espresso Bloodline
And Hear, a Moon Mermaid Rhyme
Forge your Coins, with Me Tonight

Hunting, Barista Dream
Hear that Rhyme
Mermaid just Passed By
Sailing on Moonlight

Call that Rock Star Chill
Holy Wood Smooth
Red Bull Cool
Hunting Barista Dream

Espresso High Tide
Surfing, on Blood Moon Light

Hear that Song on Mermaid Smile
And I Kindly Ask
Pour some Love

For my Thirsty Soul

Hunting Down, a Social Solitude
Charm of Street Mermaid
It's Six o' Moon Clock
Mermaid just Passed By
She's Sending Me Good Moon Vibes

'Hunting Barista Dream'

GHOST STORIES

Okay. Met *Moon Maidens* in Love, *Rome Fell*, figured out that Soul is somewhere in Heart's Atlantic Ocean, dated a bit still-so-young *Lady Ea* and spend a Pleasant Summer – good, strange journey anyways.

There are just a few more weird-to-magical things that really are insisting to be told for sake of wise of the old. If the previous ones haven't broken your healthy, artistic mind, hopefully you are still fine after Life's Ghosts hiding in odd places. But first! Just breathe smooth and think how things, and your thongs, are?

Calling my Status Quo
Lover and Poet insist
But Joker resists
King keeps his Calm
Let the philosopher do lots of Talk

Joker thinks Lover's a Big Fool
And Poet out of this World
Soldier seems to be ready for a War
But lots of political consul-tancy
Should keep him Cool

Lady thinks she Rules
But what does she know
Lover's all around her anyway
After facing the Joker's Eternal Smile
I whisper into the freedom of wind:
'Do you ever dream?'

For once
There's a Silence
In a Closed Room

Capital Cool

Why Don't You, Call it a Day?
Why Don't You, Call it a Day

Maybe the Hour is, Café Latte Cigaretto
Like a Chinese Zodiac Sign
And Quarter, Wine
Clepsydra Leaks, Red Sea to a Moon

You're Having a Meeting
Under Cap-ital Cool
Under Capital Cool

Hey Parisienne
Pantheon opening Doors and Roofs
For Poor Little Saints, Too

Why Don't You
Why Don't You?
Call it a Day
Call it a Day

Maybe the Hour, is Wine
Carrying my Colosseum
All the Appian Way

Hey Parisienne
Pour some Blood
For my Thirsty Soul

Hear that Distant Sound
They Gonna Throw my Little Socrates
Speak Wisdom to Caesar's Lions
O' Poor Little Peter
Life's a Circus Maximus, in a VIP Room

Hey Parisienne, Please
Can I Have my Capital Cool?
In a Glass, with some Vatican Mood
Maybe the Hour is Just Fine
Like the Chinese Zodiac Sign

Dopamine Cigarette

Smoking, Natural Instinct, Fear
Devil, Drive Your Ducati Please
Spin your Salsa Hips, Dear-Darling Red

Smoking, Dose of Dopamine
Burning, Shadows of Death, Under Skin
If it's Senseless, It's Meaningless

Calling my Zensei
Eagle Nose, One-Eye
If It's Senseless, It's Meaningless

And the Wise One Says
Levitate, with Her Holiness
Shiver of the Soul
Cold Rush of the Blood
Remember
Sharing Smiles with Hangman's Blue
He Never Grows Old

O' my Cigarette called Fear
Smoking Dopamine, Crystal Clear
Shadows of Adrenaline
Angel Death Fades Away

Calling my Zensei, Fear
Eagle Eye, Arrow Nose

Once, You're a Mountain
Viewing down an Ocean
Once You Grow Wings
And Take Your Chance

And the Wise One Says

Burn your Vanities
        On Bonfire of Fear
Smoking
        Cigarette of Dopamine
            Shadows of the Red Devil

If it's Senseless, It must be Meaningless

Used to Be Cool

Houston! I See a Moon

O', I Used to be Cool
  I Used to Be Smooth
    Used to, Rule the Hood

I Used to Be Cool
  Used to Do Things
    Used to, Play with the Old Fool
  Wake a Light Rain, from a Clear Blue Sky
    Used to Have, Cloud Mirror
      On Sunset Horizon

O' I Used to Be Capital Cool
  Hollywood Smooth, Diplomacy Dude
    Light as Wind, and Bright as Star
  Used to Be, Closest to the Moon
    Tide Sunglass Moods

O' I Used to be Cool
  Something like Cannes Smooth
  Used to Chase Mermaid Smiles
    On Lovely Trails, of Moon Maids

  Dive on Cliffside, Swim on Thunderstorm

Used to Take my Chance
  Roll the Dice, Run Every Street
    Used to Be Last, Leaving Eve on Beach
  Used to Trust, only on Fool's Luck
    On Fool's Luck
      Jungle Smooth, Snowfall Cool

O' I Used to Be Caribbean Cool

Smile, Hollywood Smooth
Used to Chase, Mermaids on Moonlight
Sleep under Star-Sights

Used to Be Cool
Try new Things, Play with Old Fool
Used to Be Young Soul, Ocean Smooth
King of Coolest Movie-star Dudes
Breathe of Mid-June

O' I Used to Be Cool
Used to Be Cool, Ice-Smooth

Cerveza for my Shadow

Cerveza, Por Favor
  Kasimir Calls
    It's a Geyser, on Atlantic Shore

Uno Cerveza, Por Favor
  Cold as Winter Night
    Cold as Dead of Winter Night, Please

Cerveza, Please
  Brown Sweat Tease
    Devil Tears, for my Shadow Ghost
  Geyser Blows
    Deep Drums Beneath
    Beat of the Earth

Uno Cerveza, Por Favor
  Brown Sweat Ease
    Devil Tears, Healing my Wounded Ghost
  Ice Cold, Glacier Smelts

  She's Cool, She's Delight
    She's a Bird Song
      Humming Beat of Ocean Wave

And All The Roses Fall
    All the Roses Fall
  Devil Cries, on a Summer Night

Uno Cerveza, Please
  It's Cold, It's a Delight
    Brown Sweat, Tempts my Soul
  She's Green, She's Fresh
    She's Queen, of all Palm Trees

And All the Roses Fall
        All the Roses Fall
    When Devil Cries for your Heart Tonight

Geyser Blows
    Whistles Deep Down Atlantic Soul
        Devil's Tears, Keeping my Ghost Alive
    Uno Cerveza. Please
        Green Sweat Tease

And All the Roses Fall
    Devil Cries Till Midnight

Middle-Class Monkey

I Saw a Cave Dream
Man, Sweat and Tanned
Seen Ein-Stein
Hanging, on Ocean Cliffside

I'm nothing But a Middle-Class Monkey
But mi Chimp, Jesus the Super-Star

You See
Bananas, Hanging allover a Pine Tree

I Saw a Cave Dream
Juliet, Kissing her Lover-Boy African

Bananas, Growing Upside-Down

I'm a Middle-Class Monkey
Caveman Romeo

I saw a Cave Dream
Bananas, Growing on a Melon Tree

And Juliet, African-Heart
Hugging my Friend Gorilla
Super-Hero F. Gozilla

I'm a Social Dreamer
Just a Middle-Class Monkey
But my Friend, King of Africa
Sitting on Thrown of Coconuts

Yeah, I'm Just a Middle-Class Monkey
But mi Banana, Wanna-Be Super-Star Romeo

And I Saw a Good Cave Dream
*   Juliet, Wearing only Tree Leaf*
*   Me and Ein Stein Junior*
*   Hanging Upside-Down, On Ocean Cliffside*
*   Caveman Romeo, on Sonata Lullaby Banana*

Saw a Good Cave Dream
*   Bananas, Growin' Upside-Down Again*

Six O'Moon Clock

It's Six Moon O'Clock
*   On a Planet Strange*
Distance, to You
*   Feels so Weird, and Faraway*

Been a Dry Season, for a Lifetime
*   And it's a Long Way Home*

Growing, Grapes for All
*   Guess, it's Soul Tree*
*   Singing, in a Storm Rising*
*   Plenty of Fruits, to Fall*
*   Plenty of Fruits, for All*

Six O'Moon Walks By, Freezes Time
*   Chills Landscape, Strange and Faraway*
Distance to mi Lady
*   Feels so Weird*

Been Dry Season
*   Walking with Dust Devils, too Long*

Hear a Mermaid Voice, on a Night's Void
*   Have a Hunch, it's my Soul Tree*
*   Loosing its Mind, for Awhile*
*   Howling, in a Rising Storm*

Been a Dry Season, for a Life Long

And the Distance, to a Young Moon
*   Feels so Weird*
*   Feels so Innocent and Strange*

It's Six O'Moon

On a Planet Strange
    It's a Long Way to Graveyard

Been a Dry Season, for a long
    Dust Devils Grew Tall
        Plenty of Fruits, Drying on Soul Tree

Hear a Mermaid's Voice
    Mixing my Conscious Mind
    And the Distance to mi Lady, Feels so Faraway
        And a Young Moon, Walks in your Arms
            Climbs on your Shoulders
It's Six O'Moon Clock
    On Planet Strange, Faraway

Soul Feeding

Feeding my Soul
With Innocent's Thoughts
Feeding my Fading Ghost
With Aphrodite's Cat's Moon Walks

Dreaming, Valleys of Fallen Rome

Feeding my Soul, Feeding my Soul
With Apollo's Eyes
Great Blinds, Rolling Blue Dice
Say Hi
Sister Moon, Gliding-by
She's Dreaming
All the Time Lost, in Speaking
Worthless Lips Healing

Feeding my Fading Ghost
Feeding my Fading Ghost
With Aphrodite's Lost Words
Never Thought
It was going to Be You
Killing Me, in Lover's Dream

Feeding my Soul
With Love, Starving Alone
Marching my Army of Fools
On Mistress' Dream Boots

Feeding my Fading Ghost
With Aphrodite's Lost Eyes
In Game of Love, in Disguise

Dreaming, on Apollo's Blind
Dreaming, on Apollo's Blind Again

On Valleys of Fallen Rome

Feeding my Soul
With Innocent's Thoughts
Never Thought
It was going to Be You
Killing Me, in Aphrodite's Game

O' Goddess, Eat me Alive
Eat me Alive
Save my Soul, Save my Fading Ghost

Two Dogs Bar

It's Been Dry Season
  Only God Knows How Long
  Making my Way, Over the Mountains
    Through Desert Graveyards

On the Edge of the World
  Sign Says: 'Two Dogs Bar'
O' How Thirsty We Are

Lady Shares a Smile
  'Dry Camel Tongue', Only Drink We Have
Two Dogs, Barking on the Doorway
  O' How Thirsty We Are

Next to You
  Man's Doing Mental Yoga
    With the Last Beer on Earth
There's Unsolved Mystery
  With the Shakespeare Skull
    Pandora's Jar, still Half-Full of Hope

Then Something Happens
  Memory Lost, for 20 Minutes
    When your Head Wakes-up, Got Explained
You're an Underground Field Agent
  With Traumatic Love Life
    Got Caught, and Drugged
    And Now Facing ... King of Africa, Himself
You're Speaking, Sub-Saharan Savannah
  O' My Dark Soul Old – Magnificent View

King of Africa, Whispers Smiles
  Speaks with Old Wind, Jungle Ghost
    Should You Speak What's on your Soul?

King of Africa, Tasting Scent of my Blood

Maybe, They Tell How to Live
Maybe, They Tell How to Breathe
Maybe, They Tell How to Die

Two Dogs, Barking on Doorway
Statue in the Middle of Graveyard
Holds up the Sky
Lady in Black Shares Smiles
It's the only Drink We Have Here
O' God, How Thirsty We Are

Hiding Under Sombrero

Hiding, Under My Sombrero
   Could Be Anywhere, In Time
Sunglass Shade
   Life's a Movie, Anyway

Tres Desperados, Hunting my Soul
   But I'm Fading, Under a Tequila Tree

Once a Lady, Told Me a Strange Story
   Cross-Fingered Secret, on my Heart
     She Whispered Old Magic, into my Ear
In the End, She Asked
   You Wanna Be Lost, or Found?
Since Then, Have Been Hiding
   With the Magic and Mystery

Hear That Horse Riding
   Haunted Searching Pieces of my Soul
     Secret Magic, and Lady's Lost Words
Snake Skin Boots, Sunglass Shades
Hiding, Under my Sombrero
   O' You Fools, Can't Find Me Here

Once Upon a Time
   Got Caught, Beaten, Soul Half Stolen
I Guess, Was Broken Somewhere
   And Now, I Can See Pieces of It
     Lying Everywhere, Lying Everywhere

O' Tres Desperados
   Hiding Under my Sombrero
     Fading, Under my Tequila Tree

Hear That Horse Riding

Snake Skin Boots, Sunglass Shade
Hiding Under my Sombrero

125

Been Waiting

I've Been Waiting
  Million Years
    My Bones Been Growing
And Here We Are
    Cutting Edge of Time

I've Been Waiting
  I've Been Waiting

Lain on Stone
    Dreaming on Ocean Floor
      Ages Down, Misty Dawn

Been Waiting, Billion Years
  Someone Like You
      Someone, Reading Fires of Stars

Billion Years
  Sun Been Burning
      Great Spider Planning
All Thousand Years
    I've Been Waiting
      Standing Tall, on Rain to Come

Been Waiting
  Grown Birds from my Leaves
    Talked to a Moon
        So Long, She Started Following
  Been Waiting, Someone Like You
      Someone Feeling Star Fire
      On Neural System

Billion Years, Sun Been Burning
  Great Spider Been Web Planning

I've Been Waiting
I've Been Waiting

127

LITTLE MOODIES

Double Espresso

Double white espresso
On Chinese porcelain
Smoking down ... Thirsty Soul

Cigarette

A cigarette, and a thought
A smoke, and a beauty ... for a view
God, a slow guillotine, please
An edge of the world

Boys of the Hoods

Walking on a Street of Thinking Trees
On a Slow River
Future Passes By
Wake-up, Stone Heart
What Language Do You See?

Hey, Lone Survivor
Always
On Edge of World

Castle Soul

Trembling Down Stairs
Castle Soul
Star Dust Ruins
Breathing Centuries

Say Hey
Face of World
Eye on Open Hand
Walking, Blind Man Lands

Light and Shadow
Light and Shadow
Spell my Name

Mademoiselle Earth

God Damn
Sunlight and Gravity
Reviewing my Soul

O' Mademoiselle Earth
Your Magnetic Field, and Thermal Radiance
Feeling My Mood

O' Star Boy
Just Water & Soil
Wind Bending a Rain-Bow
O' Sky Girl
So Soft, Angel Cruel – Light & Cool
Snow Dancing Down, Paradise Hood

Theater

Looking through
    Images of You
  All the Roles you Wear
     Things you Care
       And Faces you Share
  Life, you Dare
     The Theater, you Speak and Hear

French Cold

It's French Cold
   Napoleon on a Saddle
      All the Flowers on the Garden, Shiver Blue

Walking Her Vagina

Lady
   Giving her Vagina, a Walk
     Cat, So Smooth
       Steps, Slow-Mo
  Tiger Queen
    In a Jungle Deep
      Wild Cat, on Path to Moon

Lady, Walking her Va-China
   On Gardens of Eve
      Cat Super Smooth, Steps Slow-Mo Danger
  Tiger Queen Hungry
    In a Jungle War
      Wild Cat Dancing
        Invincible Shadows of Moon

Lady, just a Walk in Park, with a Little Noah's Ark

Bullet

It's like a Bullet
   Coming to You
But now
    You see it
      And can't just Move
Sir, Certain Death
   Running Over, Your Gene Pool
Run, Run you Fool

The Day you Die

The Day you Die
   The Day you Live
     And the Day, you were Born
Holy Ghost, Just Walking Through

All the Fake Roles
    In your Wardrobe
Speak to me, Silent One
   Speak to Me, Silent One

Money for Nothing

Money for nothing
   Coins raining down
    Out of free skies
Iron of your blood
   Piling and growing

Silver bars, rising on surroundings
Air, now, looking you down

Money, for nothing

Opium

Deep into the Opium, I Dive
Into a Night Sky
Stars, Falling By
Came to Say, Goodbye

Remember Me

Remember Me
Remember Me
When You're Gray and Old
Remember Me
When You Think Everything is Done, and Told

Remember me, Old Friend
Remember me, Air-Born
Remember me, Young Heart
Free Spirit, Wandering Round the World
Remember me, Blue-Eye Night-Sky

Remember me, Rainmaker
Ocean Wave, Wind-Riser

Remember me, Sun the Star
Moon Swing, Earth Spin
Remember my Name
Cast a Shadow of Soul
Tell the Tale

Down Town

Hey, my Old Friend
Come Down, Here and Slow
It's been a While
Since the Last, Social Deep Dive

Just a thought
You Splitting Eve Air
In the Middle, Earth
Makes my Philosopher, Dance
That Ancient Wave
Rhythm, so Live

Hey Come Down, Please
A Castle High
Walls Fallen, Town's Heart
Take it Ease

Fool's Stairs
Never Ending
Find Your Peace
Back to the Beginning

Hey Highness, Come Down Please
Share Your Shine, With Me
It's an Evil Deed
Dividing Belief

And if I would belong to the Ones
Born with White Wings
Would Join the Sky
With the Birds Screaming Town Roof by

Soul Wood Carves

Need to Under-Stand
How your Soul Wood
Carves
In a Mood Wind

Need to Feel
How its Leaves
Swing
On a Moon Spring Storm

Need to See
How your Ghost Shadows
Dance
In a Rain of Time

Never

A poem, never written
A life, never lived
And a red river
Running, through your Heart

Apollo,
   Bowing a Poem
   After a Shadow of your Heart
      On your Soul Wood Chest

And,
   A Whisper in a Wind
      Tells a Name
         Only Cupido Should Know